The Italian

GREY GOWRIE was born in Dublin in
ally engaged in England and the US/
until 1983 when he moved to the Welsh Marches. He taught English
and American Literature at Harvard and University College London. In
1972, on publishing his first collection of poems, he exchanged an
academic career for business and public life. He has been a company
chairman, a Cabinet minister, Chairman of the Arts Council of England
and Provost of the Royal College of Art. His previous volume, *Third
Day: New and Selected Poems*, was a Poetry Book Society Recommenda-
tion and a Book of the Year in the *Guardian* and the *Observer*. He is
married to the German journalist Adelheid von der Schulenburg and is
a Fellow of the Royal Society of Literature.

Also by Grey Gowrie from Carcanet Press

Third Day: New and Selected Poems

GREY GOWRIE

The Italian Visitor

CARCANET

First published in Great Britain in 2013 by
Carcanet Press Limited
Alliance House
Cross Street
Manchester M2 7AQ

www.carcanet.co.uk

A CIP catalogue record for this book is available from the British Library

ISBN 978 1 84777 232 9 (paper) / 978 1 84777 261 9 (cased)

The publisher acknowledges financial assistance from Arts Council England

Supported by
ARTS COUNCIL
ENGLAND

Typeset by XL Publishing Services, Exmouth
Printed and bound in England by SRP Ltd, Exeter

For
Heathcote, Brer and Malise Ruthven

Contents

I
The Andrians

II
The Italian Visitor

III
Fado Poems and a Ballad

IV
A Kensington Vespers

V
Nursery Rhyme for Ninety

VI
Memoir

I

The Andrians

for Alexander Goulandris
i.m.
Leonidas Goulandris

They fought the enemy, we fight
fat living and self pity.
                Marianne Moore

Preface

The Andrians is an elegy, a lament for a friend: the Greek painter and shipowner, Leonidas Goulandris (1927–2009). It is dedicated to another friend, Leonidas's twin brother, Alexander (Aleko). A third Greek art collector and shipowner, also a native of the island of Andros, George Embiricos, was older. He has died since the poem was written, in his nineties. The poem is also an elegy for the Cold War, the nuclear stand-off between Soviet Russia and the Western Powers, principally the USA.

The Goulandris brothers' lives, and my own, were governed by the Cold War. They were also hugely affected by the preceding 'hot' war, which we were too young to have served in. The Western economies grew, vigorously. They needed oil, and the Goulandris and Embiricos 'great seaslug tankers' shipped it around the world. Shipping charges are linked to unloading, so cargo would often appreciate while in transit. I was in no way involved in this lucrative business, although the firms I worked for derived benefit from buying and selling works of art. Most of the great Greek shipowning families were keen art collectors. But I too depended on the stalemate peace and prosperity which the Cold War allowed. I am the first generation in my paternal family not to have served, and usually fought, in the military. Our species lived dangerously (and from the point of view of the health of most other species perhaps criminally) between 1945 and 1989, the year of the fall of the Berlin Wall. But in the West even those not making fortunes were able to share in the prosperity (free higher education, for example) and pursue life and liberty as we saw fit. We were spoiled children in a way our own grandchildren will not be.

Poems register ambiguities. *The Andrians* is an ambivalent lament for our time in the sun.

The Andrians

In our rooms, our heads,
Aleko and Leonidas,
childhood twins played
wild celestial rounders
in which the otherworld
aliens of Andros
kicked, bowled, served, threw
quoits of interplanetary
debris, star fragments
hardened by Earth
for us to hit out of bounds
of this galaxy or the next.
Us: Ursus Major
and Minor and me.
In my room, my head,
I share a childhood
ten years before time
with yours; another island,
country-sized, Ireland,
with one of the Cyclades.
I break, Leonidas,
long drawn out days
of mourning *omertà*,
miss our long lunches
at Montpeliano
now you and all
the dead are 'beyond
succour and hospitality'
and risk twenty years'
devotion to trace
on a map of islands
a burned, elegiac,
musical mantra
in hopeless hope
of arming the survivor.

Though anyone born,
as we three were,
mid-20s to mid-40s
of the twentieth century

of the cross is governed
less by actuality
than an idea of world war,
the shadow moves
into every room.
You had an edge: voices
irredeemably male
by the time Greece fell.
Mother was adamant.
One leaves one's house
in town, in Athens,
neither for Turks nor,
absolutely, for Germans.
Father fell in, as usual.
It was cold. There was not
enough to eat. The Germans
scarfed what there was.
Leonidas caught frostbite.
The worst was watching,
from our miserable security,
people, other children,
hauled dead from hunger,
indifference down streets
in commandeered carts
and wheelbarrows: some
of them ours no doubt.
The Acropolis stored
grain behind barbed wire.
Andros seemed far
as Formosa, travel was
verboten and in any case
the British stole our boats.
That, in the end,
is what saved us of course.

October '44
Stalin winked at Churchill
and handed him Greece.
Sixty years, still counting,
great seaslug tankers
oil all the wheels
of our world by crawling
over the seven seas –
Ras Tanura, Mobile, Milford Haven.

The world cannot get enough
or pay enough.

Aleko,
think of the paintings!
Picassos, Pollocks, Bacons,
world-shrinking Giacomettis,
a long lovely girl by Modigliani:
spoils of peace and freedom
whose worth, when you think of it,
is only what other people think
it might be. Inestimable
beacons of valueless value,
may they sustain you.

My war was spent
heroically in de Valera's
Dublin or an empty hotel
in Co. Clare where the Shannon
slouches towards the Atlantic
to mingle with submarines.
Father, Rifle Brigade in Africa,
bored by changing for dinner
in the middle of a war,
joined the SAS. This did for him.
Behind Rommel's lines
he ran into Italians
who shot then spent a week
trying to save him.
It is our century's paradigm
of care and cruelty:
tanks and ambulances,
bullets and saline drips.
(His father, the VC,
narrowly shaved: Gallipoli.)
I knew he was there, in heaven.
Oddly miniaturised, reptilian,
my heaven, Hieronymus's hell,
fashioned at low tide
by an Irish estuary,
crawled with immortals.
I knew I would trap, stroke him
reborn as frog or water-beetle,
safe among the reeds at Killaloe.

Death died when his father-in-law,
Grandfather and I, in Wellingtons,
netted a stickleback.

On a map
where you two were,
in Athens, slightly torn,
hid by the back stairs,
Greece too looked torn.
Islands were bits of plaster
fallen off the walls of Asia
or thrown in mythic,
synthetic, unsympathetic
rage by a blind god
into a sea too shallow,
too small, Aleko, to sink them.
From a few miles out
the dovecotes of Andros
look like fortresses.
Those aliens, intergalactic
summer storm creatures,
drawn from Puck or Ariel
rather than sci-fi
or even *The Odyssey*,
clocked a few aces
back in the mid-1930s
versus Castor and Pollux.
Weapons forged for them
as nations mauled each other,
undreamt by the armourer
we met in a schoolroom,
slow-footed Hephaestos,
proved quite visionary
in the end: ultrasound,
laser beams, radar blips,
Attic Morse and worldwide
webs right out of this world.

Are things so
utterly different now?
If you Google the island
as we prepare to leave it,
as Leonidas has left it,
forever, slipping away

politely into that other
dimension which, no surprise,
is fictional like this one,
there lies Andros. None other.
Allow – what? – fifty years
of peace, south of Macedonia
at least; allow for the awful
clothes of comfort culture
(worse in Crete or Corfu):
men in shorts and sandals,
women topless with
peeling, unappetising
red lobster bosoms
likely to catch a crab;
allow all that migration
of lemming northerners
and the rise of English,
a nasal touristic whine
not pebbly vocables
ancient as sea-dark wine;
allow for the fatuity
of pizza beside *this* sea
and still there are Andrians
to infiltrate, admire:
black-eyed, heartfelt men;
black-eyed, luminous women
zoomed in on by the mind
from satellite or star.

Our own children
live today in the thick
of what seems actuality
but their children know better.
The world is not what you make
of it but what you make up.
They gaze at screens, shades
programmed to interact
with them: TVs, VDUs
now you can wave at, talk to;
Ali Baba or Babi Yar,
history and poetry,
tragedy and comedy
no longer masks but on key,
on tap when you need them.

Dressing up as a sheep
to escape mortal hurt
from an unreasoning
monocular giant is just
another video game
at the other end of the cave
or other side of the grave.

Dying
is seldom heroic
but what leads up to it
may be. Your identity,
Leonidas, your beautiful
lost butterfly blown
thousands of miles to sea,
has quit Jouxtens, Gstaad,
Athens, Eaton Square
and the limewashed island
to resume a mineral life,
to chemists the birth of life.
You who lost the power
of speech before your death
are a voice: a voice to me
now and always will be.
    'Alexander,
do you fret over women
past, present, even
in dreamy future?
I do not, although I used to.
I feel like a prowler when
I approach a canvas
and guilty, which is insane,
as if to paint were a vice
fraught with old mischief.
Remember Titian called
his ducal pornography
The Andrians though I believe
drink was on his mind.
I wonder if Kandinsky
felt like me, or de Staël.
The latter topped himself
after all, in Antibes.
Later, when you are really
working you're more like a cop –

whodunnit? who's going to do it? –
or an archaeologist. You look for a sign
in the sand before the waves
gently obliterate…'
   'Don't worry.
I will anchor your sign
or put to sea without you.'
     'That, in any case.'

Dying seldom heroic,
  pain is the real thing
and loss. Pain calls upon
great chords of courage.
When Achilles' spear
took Hector in the throat
it shaved the windpipe
thereby allowing them both
a terrific, all–stops–out
proto–Verdi duet.
My wife's father, unspeakably
murdered at Plötzensee,
spirits a letter home.
Even in retrospect
you pray for him to find
fulfilment in his fight
for air and decency.
Mine wanted to send
a message before he died –
to my mother? to his mother?
to his sons? his CO?
There was no pen
and he spoke no Italian.

Giordano Bruno,
  your hero, Leonidas,
strove like you to make signs
from systems and vice versa.
Fire, earth, water, air
moved, as they do, and so
were subject to geometry.
This puzzled Protestants,
enraged the Inquisition
who tied him to a stake
in Rome, at Campo dei Fiori,

strewn with sticks not flowers,
and set them alight.
It was the seventeenth
of February, 1600
and in that same year
on the second of August
John, Earl of Gowrie,
famous too for magic
(we call it science),
was stabbed with his brother
as a creditor of the King;
the bodies quartered, hanged –
posthumously, thank God.
Bruno's unthinkable pain
and what they wanted to do
to John and to the Master
of Ruthven, the brother,
rebuke our own exit.
We three were just spoiled
children of Cold War,
freed by nuclear stand-off
between eagle and bear
(sixty years! it may end
in tears and proliferation)
to follow life and liberty
and happiness without
being put to the question.
Now an age may no longer
smooth over suffering,
ice melts and the seas
weep. The Wall came down;
with it our world. Aleko,
Leonidas, your world
and mine – for our kind
more ways of ending
than one. East will move west
over again, south north.
But always there is the island
and an encroaching sea.

If Giordano
was right, signs are significant
themselves as well as faithful,
for a time at least,

to what they signify.
On a flight to Paris
Aleko crossed himself
as I did. He was up front,
open to that instrument
of hope and torture,
the truer witness.
We were visiting
Mrs O'Metty – was that David
Sylvester's joke or Beckett's?
She stared at us in real
space, identical
with scratchy oils and drawings
all over Aleko's walls.
When I swim in Aleko's pool
Bacon's *John Edwards*
presides: identical,
again. The masters distort
in verisimilitude
of life itself, its quantum
flux and tremor.
We have come to know
Françoise and Marie-Thérèse
as well as our own girls.
Magic we do not believe in
starts to come true
in diagrams. When you draw lines,
Leonidas, between the stars
from wherever you are standing
when you look up at night
in the Cyclades or the un-
lightpolluted plateaus
of the high Sahara,
you capture the likeness of signs.
You get them. You did, Leonidas,
get them: often, usually,
but never enough for you.
So you return.

Your Neapolitan
found stars immeasurable
solar systems – with planets?
with people? – lonely
seamarks of Renaissance

yet Christocentric thought,
like 'Through the light
which shines in natural
beings one mounts upward
to the light which presides
over them.' Remember Wallace
Stevens' President ordaining
the bee to be immortal, all
our centuries on? Bless
such men.

I hope one does
mount upward, Leonidas.
Not because that is tenable
but because the harbingers
are come, the forerunners,
and you are one of them.
One for your twin brother
and for me. I think of you,
dead, as a point of light;
will you to illumine
us and heal us a little
as the shamans do.
Try to illumine your twin.
Losing one is worse
than any death: a bio-atrocity;
half your soul fled; a terror.

Your lucky thirties
fell in the 1950s:
the Ike-bound, chainsmoking
post-war recovery years.
You and Aleko made
the world go round and gained
its bounty. Remember Ten Forty
Fifth Avenue, floating above
the centre of Central Park?
One could almost glide
on canvas down to the Met.
Martinis, Taittinger at 6pm;
Benny Goodman playing *Avalon*
on the just-invented stereo.
How electric to build,
re-build a family fortune,

multiply it like dreams:
the seaslugs crawling;
Ras Tanura, Mobile, all
conduits to Milford Haven;
Clausewitz; plain arithmetic;
keeping quiet; scuppering a bid.
(Soon your successor
may be carrying water
in the 21st-century
famine wars).
You were the masters
of that universe
when I was nineteen
and spent my Long Vac
on Sappho's Lesbos, Mytilene.
I lived like a lord
on a quid a day.
Ouzo cost sixpence, beer
four shillings but you got
whitebait and fried eggs,
feta, lamb's liver,
bread, olives, sustenance
thrown in with each bottle.
I hired a donkey.
You died before
I could tell you about it,
Leonidas.

I wish I'd had
time to tell you.
We say goodbye
to the body, that capsule
of anxiety and desire,
are left with a traveller
in space, an alien,
a calm illusory ghost
for conversation.
Your friend and rival,
the corsair genius
George Embiricos,
and fellow Andrian,
suffers your passing.
I imagine us now,
another trio,
talking to you also.

Old gods dance
in cyberspace, astral pals.
Apollo 13 caught a glimpse
of the Mediterranean.
All that far-off undergraduate
summer I did nothing
for days but watch a wind
off Troy ruffle waves
up and down and over
the pebbled shore,
watch the old men
squat on pebbles, beat
squid caught that morning
against them, all day
slap, bash, for supper,
up and down, all day
beating over and over
squid on the grey stones

       to make them tender.

II

The Italian Visitor

Preface

I was born at the very end of a decade, W.H. Auden's 'low dishonest' one: the 1930s. So my life accords tidily with the journalistic habit of thinking in decades. I am a Forties child, a Fifties teenager, a young adult in the Sixties and so on. Recently, I embarked on a sequence of poems about childhood. Though the world war did impinge on childhood, especially its effects on the grown-ups, my most acute memories are of its immediate aftermath. There was an odd conjoining of relief and celebration with grieving (my father was killed in action in his twenties), rationing, drab austerity, cold.

Coincidentally, while working on the sequence, I read Jonathan Galassi's great bilingual edition of Eugenio Montale's poems. Montale visited Britain two, perhaps three times in 1948. I noticed that a master poet and an apprentice (I versified the way other children drew) were twice in that year within a few miles of each other. I thought I might 'throw' my childhood: objectify it, by entering into a conversation, in old age, with a dead master. So these poems, which I call transcriptions, have been prompted by, not rendered from, their great originals.

The first, 'Eastbourne', was written about the time my parents met and I came into being as an idea. My version introduces two historical figures: the then Duke of Devonshire, who owned much of Eastbourne, and Montale himself. 'Black Trout' and 'Argyll Tour' find the great poet and the eight-year-old boy in the same parts of the island at the same time and in the same year. 'Crescent Wind' and 'Ely' are written as if spoken by Montale. They are, however, much more English: less allusive, less hermetic than the originals. 'Metropolitan Christmas' is my own memory of the grown-up world during the Christmas that followed my ninth birthday. Again, I introduce Montale as a character. The link between us was not only time and place. We were both T.S. Eliot groupies. Seven years later, in my mid-teens, I stalked Eliot during school half-term holidays. I didn't want to speak to him, or get his autograph. I wanted him simply to be there, like the recently conquered Everest. Montale celebrated Eliot's sixtieth birthday, which fell in 1948. Eliot won the Nobel Prize for Literature in that year; Montale won it in 1975. 'Syria' is an 'imitation', in Robert Lowell's sense of the word. I have tried to offer an equivalence in English of a very beautiful (and topically haunting) poem. As is only appropriate, the sequence begins and ends, therefore, with 'the Italian visitor', not me.

Eastbourne

The Duke of Devonshire taps his boiled egg
in a seaside bay window of the Grand
Hotel. In the hall, men from a military
or ex-military band unpack and start to lug
their instruments up to the little gazebo
at the end of the pier. Brass catches the sun.
The front begins to fill with Bank Holiday
people and donkeys. The sea is calm this morning;
the duke restless, a touch put out.
He has dreamed for what he thinks was all night
(just a couple of seconds) of a violin waltz
danced, in his own ballroom, by the Lord
President of the Council, i.e. Mr Baldwin,
and Agatha Christie. He blames the newspapers,
fears capital taxes and the end of his line.
Sun and the white and gold of his brown egg
cheer him: all that buttered toast.
He calls for his man and the dog to accompany
his walk with a cigar along the beach,
apocalypse postponed. The band plays
God Save the King, softly, to warm up,
make no one stand to attention.
                                    Waves from France
curl in, lazy. It is 1933
or 4. Nothing bad will happen
quite yet; a few years hence the very worst…

As the duke leaves, an unaccompanied
grey-eyed gentleman in a grey suit
folds his napkin, heads in the same direction.
He has to be foreign: the cut of the suit.
French or Italian. He looks of an age
with His Grace and in the middle of the way.
He too has dreamed all night: two women
waltzing together, in frayed silk,
somewhere a long way off, the Roseland Ballroom
in New York perhaps; one dark, one fair;
not talking; both a bit emblematic
for his taste and no doubt bored by each other.
They leave him fretful. He needs the sea.

Electric trains bring a badly dressed crowd
from London. Vendors in caps display
industrial confectionery and ice cream
that horrifies the man in the grey suit.

Now all is clear.

He is indeed Italian: Genovese.

Here come the elderly, companions
pushing wheelchairs, the crippled
by money not the war wounded.
Through revolving doors of the Grand Hotel
and its siblings children shout their laughter,
turn all day in paradisal circles.
Waves play piano on the pebbled shore
until drowned out by the band, in full voice
now with Sousa, *The British Grenadiers,*
The Eton Boating Song, Men of Harlech.
Eastbourne's en fête: a *Ferragosto*
for protestants, unbelievers, dukes.
Ice stopped not far from here.

The grey Signor

listens only to armies marching
to the full bass thump, the irritable snare,
the what-to-do, what-to-do of a trombone,
marching through Europe and across the sea.
Time, pretty soon, *pro patria mori.*
He wonders if passion is historical.
Was there ever more to the Trojan war
than Helen or Briseis?

What girl will put out the lights

of Europe? What girl cross the Atlantic?
Vince il male… La ruota non s'arresta
he murmurs but the merry-go-rounds are turning
in this sunny town, waiters staring
out of the windows of wedding-cake hotels,
the British frowning with all their concentrated
rage to have fun and it is still Bank Holiday.

Black Trout: Reading 1948

How odd, how consolingly weird,
that a writer seeking an image for his love
chose a black trout, in the river Thames, at Reading:
polluted town of gravel and biscuitry.
Ancient bream or predatory pike
perhaps; seldom that lithe elated flail.

After the war, in bankrupt utilitarian
England the boy lived a few miles downstream
at Windsor. The King used to come to tea
with anxious protuberant eyes and controlled stammer.
At ease with children, he told his equerry
to slip him a shilling. Sweets were still 'on the ration'.
Major Thing had half-a-crown only – more than double –
and whispered that he was doing well.
                            The Governor, a VC,
and His Majesty took a turn round the Moat Garden
with pipe and gasper, to give privy counsel and get it.

If only, *maestro*, you had rented a car,
driven a few miles south, to Stratfield Saye, say,
and the Loddon, or a few miles further, and the Test,
retired officers, some quite badly wounded,
would have kitted you out for the piscatorial
challenge of all time: stalking a pound-and-a-half
wild brown trout with red iridescent markings
and silver belly: an individual you spotted
hours before and among long wavering grasses
and treacherous cast-catching willows floated your false
irrelevant insect, more nuisance than food,
from a waxed line to dance less than an inch
in front of his sneering mouth; then judged the second
between his taking it in and spitting it out
to strike with your Hardy, strike, but not too hard...
You would have earned your metaphor, your tight lines
to win that far-off, faintly identified
woman and ease her into the open creel
of your heart.
                            The Test, *padrone*, not the Thames.
Clear waters well from chalk, not muddy clay
as the boy knew, and might have taken you in hand.

Argyll Tour: Glasgow 1948

Rich and poor circle
the ship-building city
like gulls who feed
off anything: cigarette
butts; toffee paper; even,
it's said, the eyes of sheep
driven down hills to queue
in front of an abattoir.
Your Clyde sweats
oil and tar...

For a few pounds, you cover
a frenzy of islands; for a few more,
hire your own man to show you
harbour life.
                    It rains a lot but the sun shines
more than they say. You know the city
is only a boat, after all; a tributary
of the Irish Sea, small sliver of the Atlantic.

Where, you ask yourself, am I going
and what can I be doing? Ossian
never spoke well to you and you never visited
Fingal's Cave on Staffa, the great Turner
in the Brooklyn Museum. America
beckons; an unbroken horse
lashes out in his pen and splinters
what's left of your heart.
                    The stable mice
find you ridiculous. Sleek liners
built in this town will carry you over the water
whenever you summon the nerve to board them.
Years later, thinking about you, I know you won't.

By coincidence we find ourselves in the same
quarter of vanished time. It is 1948.
I am eight years old, you around fifty:
timid, lovelorn, indecisive, a giant of letters.
My family want me to visit Great Uncle Hugo,
dying and still quite rich from ship broking.

I have nothing to say. He grunts and dribbles
and needs to be fed.
                    From my bedroom window
I watch seals on the beach flex their moustaches.
Weak sunsets illumine the Paps of Jura.
I long to be back on the night train from Glasgow,
comforted by the little electric blue
nightlight above my bunk on the Euston sleeper,
the rails' monotonous grind. Going home.
                            You, all over the place,
try to anchor yourself with a catalogue
of urban impressions: the canals; the ragamuffins;
clatter of chains as the boats cast off;
the mildewy, mushroomy smell when a squall passes;
a vagrant's laugh or cry and everywhere
shadows of gulls with their intermittent screaming,
the song that money sings, and no money.
                         At ten o'clock
lights come on, gulls start to disappear,
quills of smoke rise from rationed coal.
It won't wash. You know perfectly well
you need a name and the face and the body
                                 to put to that name,
emerge through the foreign gloom and try to enslave you.

Crescent Wind: Edinburgh 1948

That engineering miracle, the Bridge
of Forth, will not direct me to you.
Just one look, one blink of an eye and I'll
flog through sewers of the ancient keep
or be dragged over cobbles to find you.
But like this weak sun on the veranda
my powers are about to fail.

John Knox has strayed into each spruce square
and crescent of the New Town, the enlightened city
built two hundred years after he died.
He asks me to look for God, not you.
I tell him that's much easier.
                         He shakes his head
in fury and disappears in an up-draught
of wind off the sea and a flurry of men and women,
doors, chimney stacks, pigeons: a bearded man
in a smock and a rage, like a Chagall painting.

Ely 1948

A de Havilland Dove ascends from a still–commissioned
East Anglian airfield and shakes its small
wings at all the damaged and marooned
Lancaster bombers. I watch it fly
until it is even higher than Ely cathedral,
an alp in this flat land.
                              Sky tries to sustain the little dove
a while longer and the two towers
swap sunrise and sunset. Afternoons
are flat, also, and grey: memorial services.
Cromwell and Co. hacked the noses off
shelved medieval saints. Our modern world
hums quite happily, like the de Havilland,
over the nave just now.
                              All my life I have loved the sun
and the colour of honey. Now I long for the dark
to crouch and soar in; with you, my grave, my cathedral.

Metropolitan Christmas 1948

Things sparkle: fewer
queues for bread and bacon
but then sheet ice…

Frost tidies
involuntary gardens
in the bombed lots.

Coal dust from fires
all over London
enriches a Thames sunset;

you can see why,
from his window at the Savoy,
Monet was so happy.

Mayfair flats
sport electric bars
with chrome surrounds
for heating.

They draw on dense
coal-flecked clouds
from Sir Giles Gilbert Scott's
Battersea Power Station

that loom over Carlyle
Mansions, the home
of T.S. Eliot and the crippled
scholar, John Hayward.

Chelsea Old Church
is being rebuilt
after the raid
of '41.

Death, terror, deliverance
have stayed the Almighty's
withdrawing roar.
The churches are full.

Fish – herring and salmon –
smoulder in Whitechapel
as the East End's Essex
diaspora begins.

Coal fires, tobacco
and Thames mist;
you need to grope
your way through this town.

A foggy night
on the Isle of Dogs.
The docks discharge
imperial food.

Maynard Keynes
left when his mind
caught official art
and the Stock Exchange

but Picasso will come
if only to change trains
on his way to Sheffield
and a Communist do.

Taxed and afraid
a once-ruling class
escapes to kill pheasant

while the masters now
worry that Welsh
miners will come out
and switch off the lights.

The King of Norway
donates an immense
tree for display
in Trafalgar Square.

Nelson ignores it.
Landseer's lions
guard him and sneer
at the hungry pigeons.

At Chartwell Churchill
writes up his war.
Mrs Attlee chauffeurs
her husband about.

Aneurin Bevan
defeats the doctors
but patients praise him.

(Compiling this scrapbook
in Twenty Twelve
I see I was being packed
off to boarding school.)

Coupons for clothes,
petrol, everything.
The Tories dream
of a conflagration.

Some believe
the war has been lost
now that America
must be repaid,

Poland fettered
and George the Sixth
an *R*, not *RI*.

At 10 Curzon Street
Heywood Hill
await the arrival
of *Nineteen Eighty-Four*;

East of the Elbe
one former ally
places no order.

Opposite, street
walkers are unpenned
from Shepherd Market.

You can get hold of things
if you know where to look
and whom to sleep with.
Harrods is bursting.

*

Up and down
the escalators
rides an entranced
Italian poet.

A 'lower case' Catholic
and a genius
he celebrates Eliot's
sixtieth birthday.

The copper-coloured store
is heaven to him;
the Underground
a descent into hell.

He views the women
in his life in the same
way his Science

peers view matter:
girls are different
when they are observed

and at their best
if loved under strict
laboratory conditions
like wayward particles.

With fake French accent
Madame Louise
from Clerkenwell fixes
each permanent wave.

Cosmetics? Gold.
Who would not sell
her soul for a stick
of Elizabeth Arden?

Mayfair abounds
in dressing tables
and black-market nylons

but things have changed
with the Yanks departed
and fewer maids.

Because of the open
space, for luggage,
taxi-drivers are cold
as the cabbies were.

They form a line
in Berkeley Square
for spent revellers
in starched shirts.

A pearly branch
of mistletoe
lets Uncle John kiss
his niece on her mouth.

The band is longing
to get home now.
The grey-eyed Italian
will head for Victoria

where lovely informal
plumes off steam trains
waft his heart
to the Cinque Terre.

*

After the feast
the host is gathered
and hidden away.

All that remains
is our glimpse of the eternal
and the washing-up.

Syria

The ancients say poems
are a ladder to God.
                    Reading mine,
you may harbour a few
reservations. But oh my darling,
I knew it was so that day
you gave my voice back to me,
when goats broke loose from somewhere
to slaver on thorn or marram
while clouds lost their bearings
and sun and moon exchanged
unearthly looks with each other,
and our car conked out, and only
an arrow, a scrawl on a stone,
blood red, as if written in blood,
pointed us on our way
by road to Aleppo.

after Montale

III

Fado Poems and a Ballad

Preface

In 2007 I was given lunch at the RIBA by Andrew Barnett, the London director of Lisbon's Calouste Gulbenkian Foundation. Chatting about the wonders of Portugal and the Portuguese, I mentioned how, in the 1970s, I used to dine regularly at O Fado, a Portuguese restaurant in Knightsbridge. I disliked music in restaurants, except this one. Twice each evening a female singer would give a short recital of *fado* songs, *fado* being Portugal's marine equivalent of the American South's land-locked blues.

Andrew started to scribble on a notepad. The upshot was that the Gulbenkian commissioned eighteen poets, myself among them, to do English versions, alongside the Portuguese originals, of *fado* songs. An admirable editor, Mimi Khalvati, sent everyone literal translations. Most of us read these two or three times and then riffed away textless. I kept the Portuguese titles of my three songs as their Latin texture seemed to me to contribute to the music. An anthology, *Saudade*, was published by the Foundation in 2010.

For some years, the poet-in-residence at Harvard was Elizabeth Bishop. In 2012 I happened to read that Bishop made her class write a ballad. Her own Rio de Janeiro ballad, 'The Burglar of Babylon', is one of her most arresting poems. I was appalled; I had reached an advanced age without ever attempting a ballad. I was at the time debating whether to try to render Victor Hugo's 'Booz Endormi' into my English. It is one of the most sensual and beautiful poems in French. But English is a rather literal language and 'Booz Endormi', to a literal English mind, is embarrassing in an unpleasant way if rendered into our revelatory tongue. An old man (Booz, but obviously Hugo himself) is having a sexual fantasy. Fair enough. But the fantasy is that a lovely young woman is having a sexual fantasy about him. Dream on. My ballad attempts to remove the yuckiness of this situation by turning the Ruth story into a post-feminist account of the founding of Israel.

Madrugada

Cold night with dawn breaking
like ice at the moment of waking
and your heart a dream window
you cannot look out of or know
whom to follow, where to go
and your love a shadow.

You drift on alone
through backstreets of Lisbon
empty as you are.
Is it worth walking so far
for some moral star,
for someone not there?

If only you knew
whom you wanted to make love to
in the end, or could come
to believe in the dream
she was the same
one you suspected all the time.

The time that flows down
byways of a sleeping town
as each reiterating dawn
of your life wears on
to disappoint and inspire
your song, your sad guitar.

after the Portuguese of Fernando Pinto do Amaral

Vielas De Alfama

In dead hours of night
a guitar is trembling
and a woman singing
her bitter *fado*.

Even through the grimy
and murky glass
of her window
there comes a voice
for all who go
down alleys of Alfama,
streets of old Lisbon,
hurt by her sorrow.

I wish I lived there
too, for the *fado*.
I would spy, like the moon,
on secretive lovers
half-seen in doorways
or spurred on by sad
and shameful old songs

of the streets of Alfama,
alleys of Lisbon,
the moon, the guitar
and the woman singing.

after the Portuguese of Artur Ribeiro

Lembrai-te da Nossa Rua?

Remember our street?
Where we used to meet
and lived and loved in? Where you
used to live and I still do
and which was supposed to see us through?

Cold winds came,
cold even for springtime,
to sweep you away
like leaves that fell later
the autumn after

you'd gone. A sea
in moonlight brings you back to me
sometimes, but it is only
a mirage, a stratagem,
a ghost in my garden.

Our poor street
looks empty now it is too late
to find you. Sometimes
I imagine you coming and going
like you used to. But there is only the going.

after the Portuguese of António Calém

A Ballad of Bo-oz and Ruth

Bo-oz was ancient, but a good man
    and wealthy: kine far as eye can see;
goats galore; a decent chunk of arable
    lowland made up the polity.

He meted justice in a trembly voice;
    remembered birthdays and children's names;
advanced overdue rental (once only)
    but paid for festivals, for the wine and games.

His wives were modest and he married less
    than custom or his temperament allowed.
Children and grandchildren thronged each tent,
    punished only when they got too proud

to mingle with servants or lend a hand
    with threshing and bread-making. He'd collect
tithes with a smile and a present. You treated God,
    his children and his creation with respect.

Bo-oz was a river to his people. They
    knew very well that their prosperity
and dull peaceful days were down to him.
    His being so old caused private anxiety.

For Bo-oz had been a terror in his time
    to anyone who threatened Bethlehem,
the Moabites chiefly. He marshalled guard
    and fought in the front line and slaughtered them.

Rage has its purpose. Long years of peace
    in Judah were founded on the sword.
Bo-oz roused had been fearful, also fearless.
    Most of his children were conceived in blood

after a battle; never, it's said, before –
    Keep off the grass, keep away from the kine
and the womenfolk. Cower in your tents
    before you covet what is God's, and mine.

He got his way and life rolled along
    in peace and fertility for a generation.
If he could only last the odds were good
    for Bo-oz to turn his tribe into a nation.

But he was no longer strong and he was lonely.
    Women still eyed him from behind their veils,
their young men grown too sluggish. Peace has its languor.
    You need spunkier men because peace fails

in the end. Bo-oz' best wife, the one who made
    him laugh and most excited him,
left him for a pain about her breast
    and all rejoicing to the Seraphim.

One summer, early in harvest time,
    two women, a mother and her daughter-in-law,
wife of a dead son, both Moabites
    fallen on hard times, knocked on his door.

Bo-oz had kept the peace but skirmishes
    and border disputes often caused affray.
Naomi, though distantly related
    to the great man, had lost both sons that way.

In hard times you must forget or bury
    a bitter past. Naomi knew that widowed Ruth
had every prospect of re-marrying
    on enemy ground. That was the bitter truth.

She sent her daughter-in-law into the fields
    to help with the harvest. She looked Bo-oz in the eye
and pleaded all the family connections.
    Bo-oz was merciful. By-and-by,

inspecting his fields, he spotted the newcomer
    gleaning his corn gracefully, yet with vim.
That night, for the first time in many years,
    a wild erotic dream was granted him.

The girl whose oval face and silky eyes
    suggested that she hailed from further north
than Moab, from the Damascenes perhaps,
    came into his tent. She swore an oath

of fealty and forgiveness, absolute
    as if before the Ark, yet with a smile
so welcoming his years all fell away
    like bedclothes. Bo–oz rose and, for a while,

time was thrown off too; the harvest night
    stayed as it was, day refused to dawn,
his sleeping wives stopped breathing. Then, the roles
    of petitioned and petitioner withdrawn,

justice and decency were cast aside
    with custom and any sense of evil.
God himself withdrew, quite tactfully.
    (Bo–oz had no concept of the devil.)

But what of Ruth? She was used to being admired.
    Gleaners had made their admiration plain
in minutes. She'd always known that power lay
    best with women who would lie with men

at times of women's choosing. Love, she knew,
    had little to do with it; time everything
and touch: how you washed their feet and when
    you fed their fancy. It helped if you could sing

softly to them also and recognise
    the child within each man. Ruth's soul was bound
in secret to one love and one love only:
    a secret she meant to take into the ground

with her body and her beauty and her skill
    at giving pleasure, and making sure.
Love worked best for woman among women;
    Naomi was the one worth dying for.

Ruth loved Naomi: for herself or through the son;
    in memory, in desire and for their plan
to thwart a partial god, who had done wrong
    to both, by Ruth seducing an old man.

Only once had she given too much away.
    'Whither thou goest, I will go,' she'd said
and *'where thou diest, will I die.'* She knew
    love is the only passport for the dead

to take into that vast eternity
    you grasp by looking up at the night sky,
especially from desert to the south and east:
    the wordless wastes that whispered *Na-o-mi*.

Back to the dream. Was it a dream? Or real?
    Did a lovely girl, amid alien corn,
so catch the imagination of an old
    warrior that from one night a king was born,

generations on, to build a land
    whose history still shakes the world today?
People have painted Ruth, and written songs,
    but the good book says she gave the babe away

to Naomi, to claim as her very own:
    a son new-born to nurse on her own breast,
a gift of love from woman unto woman;
    great Bo-oz a delivery boy, at best.

Naomi's son was King David's grandfather.
    Ruth and Bo-oz soon disappear from view.
The stars illumine still the murderous wastes
    and whisper where they go we will go too.

*Prompted by the Old Testament, Book of Ruth; John Keats, 'Ode to a Nightingale'; and
Victor Hugo, 'Booz Endormi'.*

IV

A Kensington Vespers

i.m. Pamela Fletcher (1910–2005)

Numbers

for Roy Davids

We lunge at status, buying shabby chic
plum Chesterfield sofas, out of date
Turkey-pattern carpet, false mahogany
lavatory seats and engraved writing paper.
Le bourgeois gentilhomme: the old shoe look.
Over the cistern hangs a glazed and framed,
foxed, fading, 1907 or '08
sepia photograph of my Hodgson great-uncles.
They line up in identical, four-buttoned,
three-quarter-length trousered suits as if for a sad
irretrievable event: a cricket committee
perhaps, or all-day Board of the family firm
of auctioneers, probate their specialty.
They look to be late thirties or early forties
and no wonder: all survived the First World War.
Three of the four died before '29
rang down their curtain.
                  Men of the middle sort,
minor public school, each kept households
of seven at least: cook, kitchen maid, valet, gardener,
housekeeper, maid and tweeny. They shared an itinerant nanny;
also Frl. Sorge, the governess.
                      Only last year we came upon two
sets of accounts with the photo and other stuff
in a trunk stencilled *Not Wanted On Voyage*. Median income
was £5000; given the tax pre-dating
Asquith and Lloyd George three hundred grand today.
Uncle Li had four times that, a De Dion Bouton,
a chauffeur and a mechanic; Uncle Walter,
the only one I met, who died in his nineties
the day before Labour came in, in '64,
a quarter as much, or less.
                Taking a leak, I think of England;
southern England: Hodgson homes in Dulwich, Putney,
Milford in Surrey, Angmering-on-Sea.
Ten per cent of the profit earmarked for charity,
they wintered in San Remo; Uncle Li in Cannes.
In their lives the statistical character of quantum theory

became linked to the inexactness of perception.
We climb a ladder sometimes to inspect the state
of Walter Hodgson's bequest to my twenty-four-
year-old self and run an indolent duster
across it: forty volumes of Wisden
pre-1914, custom-bound in fine Morocco.
Hobbs, who ended up with 199 centuries,
was thought quite reckless, one hundred years ago,
batting for Surrey, in a rainy season,
but the public liked it; he buckled down for the Test.
Around the time my great-uncles were being born
Marx thought bourgeois society prehistoric,
energy of British workers oozed away.
Bow-tied, blazered, en route to another appointment,
Sotheby's man said, 'Roughly? Five to seven K.'

Lines

(i)

Sam is dead
or dying – what I mean is
logic can't get *at* him any more.

(ii)

By no means hurry
but try not to worry.
Others before
you have gone through this door.

(iii)

Shit, shave and shower;
new canonical hours.
Where did the old ones go?
What happened to
'Be sure to brush your teeth and say your prayers'?

(iv)

Are souls no longer
at issue? Our souls are.
We still feel
pity and terror
in gut before mind
gets round to them.
I beseech you,
in the bowels of Christ,
not to forget the abandonment,
as well as the pain, Good Friday,
nor the joy, dropping off,
an immaculate joy
as sleep steals over,
of fading consciousness.

(v)

Tom Stoppard, in conversation:
'Laughter is the sound of comprehension.'
Tom's an OM and always on the button.

(vi)

Sam is a shit
but I'll miss him.

(vii)

After the funeral
people turn their mobiles back on
and walk among the headstones
talking.

Reece Mews

Hole in the sky
simultaneously
open and enclosed.
Reach it by locked
door, by empty
stable, carless
garage to climb
well-nigh vertical
stair, ladder even,
shinnable only by
chauffeurs, grooms:
past lives. Come
to the studio
in a dingy, cobbled
Kensington mews.
Just three rooms
off a minuscule
landing. One
shows a plump
bed by a stack
of books, a lamp
perilously perched
on top of them.
The Georgian
table has glasses
laid out; the bottle
of Krug sweetly
condensating. Thin
electric flexes
hang from ceilings
and sway a little
with footfall: bulbs,
bare naked, seen
in many paintings.
A great Louis XVI
chest houses neat,
off-duty jockey
clothes. Kitchen
doubles with bath,
less WC: the closet,

as per George Dyer's
death in a Paris hotel,
somewhere off-stage.
The bath's wood lid
has laundered grey
shirts laid on it
next to a workable
stove. After a few
thousand beaded
bubbles you enter
a small room, big
window, round
mirror reflecting
it plus ubiquitous
dreck: dust, debris,
tins and brushes,
scored photographs,
pinned Old Master
repros, Polaroid
self-portraits. Paint
splatters the walls
like a mad Saint
Valentine's Day
Massacre, only
colours of splendour.

Now, farcically,
all this primordial
chaos is re-made
in Dublin's Kilmainham
Jail, scene of English
executions; a painter's
childhood excitement.

Back in champagne-
swilling 1980s,
you see in that small
room, on unprimed
canvas, a naked man
supple enough to clean
toes of his right foot
in a hand basin:
white, suspended
in the void of days.

Pink flesh of back,
soft and muscular
as a seal, he seems
to be dancing not
washing: two nods
to the way of Degas.
That curious piping,
high register voice,
clipped, punctuated,
says, 'So few people
look, I find, at paintings.
How odd they want
to buy them.' You
have not been asked
for comment, are here
to look. Twenty years
and a death in Madrid
pass before you see
that tough and tender
Nu de dos again.
Now it hangs glazed
in a gold frame.

Reece Mews: Conversation Piece

Don't worry.
I'll send the bill to Miss Beeston.
She quite likes you, which is unusual,
as she only likes me and I suppose a few women.
It may be because I told her you helped me
not get thrown out of my studio.

Did you know Muriel?

I never went much. I am not unstuffy.
I don't mind Miss but draw the line at Cunty.
She let me off it when we met at Wheeler's
with my wife. She knew we were waiting for Israel
and told me, 'He wouldn't be late for that one.'
I knew he had died. Rang the police. They couldn't go in,
they said, but try the firemen. So I did. We went up a ladder
and there he was, on the bed, his jaw dropped,
mouth rigid and open. Clothed. The bedroom was tidy.
The rest of the flat, a large one, a waste-paper basket
version of your studio: scraps of writing on chairs,
pages torn out of books. He wanted to prove
Shakespeare was written by your namesake.

My ancestor. Or so my father said.

I liked the way he looked. I've not been frightened
since but I think I have never been frightened
of the outcome, only of the process.

I am the other way round. The process is interesting.
I used to spend a fair amount of time
on crucifixions. Pain and thirst confirm
we are alive and of course the disposition
of the limbs and the torso absorbs one.
I sleep little. Dreams are dull and childish.
It is pointless to miss the light of reality
so why sleep more than you have to?

56

We are indefinitely dead. I get all the exercise
I need in that small room when I am painting.
I never sit down. I dance about like a boxer,
feinting with the image, trying to spot
when it will come, what it is going to look like.
It's usually tosh. Just occasionally
solid appearance builds from the shadow
and all the shadow-boxing. I feel a stab
of happiness. Then I go downstairs
and visit my friends and eat and get drunk.

Look, you have tried to paint
what Eliot called 'contaminating presences'
about the human. These work better as shadows,
for me, than dragon shapes, or bats; my family
being, absurdly, associated with vampirism.
If, in the late 18th century, you wanted to write
a vampire story you called the vampire Lord Ruthven,
like Byron's pal, William Mason. It's Hollywood
compared to the great curse in *Eumenides*.
                              That art collector
I introduced you to, George, whispered it in Greek.
My hairs stood up. Not only the promised end
but an image of horror gone political.
                              Tell me about Ireland
as we have Dublin and Co. Kildare in common.

Just the idea of going there gives me asthma.
Ireland was only England when I was young
plus the Holyhead packet and an interminable train.
I told David I liked my mother and grandmother
and hated my father but found him attractive sexually.
Of course he whipped me. Or had stable boys do it.
That settled things, in a way. I don't enjoy betting on horses
because they stop me breathing. Lucian loves them.
At his boarding school he'd sneak out
at night to sleep beside one. I'd be dead by morning.

He cuts *me* dead these days. I wrote an essay
which struck me as appropriately asslicking
only I said you were an imagination, Lucian an eye.

Boringly self-evident, I'd have thought.
There it is.
                    You never painted Caroline?

Not enough definition. Wonderful eyes
but aquamarine is a sort of Memling colour
and anyway Lucian did her.
He cuts me too. I miss him.
I am thirteen years older.
He finds me repetitive, boring. I suppose I am.
Of course I drink more than he does.

More to it than that. He's a good painter
but embarrassing whenever he tries to shock:
rats nuzzling your balls and all that. You do not need
immense perception to see why he is trying.
He should stick to his line of beauty.
                            That girl from behind,
in a blue dressing gown, lying on her side,
I'd give an eye for, and the wild flowers in a Belfast sink.

Oh well I think I am a bit boring.
It's the worst thing about age. The best thing
is you can still paint. Matisse,
whom I've never much gone for, says painting's an old man's game.
Picasso did all those dreadful Delacroix
but Jacqueline pissing is a masterpiece.
                            I have asked John
to meet us at Wiltons. He likes you too.
Do not flatter yourself. He is a snob.
Extraordinary that you're paying. I suppose
you are on a expense account. I warn you,
I'm an expensive guest.

I draw the line at Lafite or Mouton
also. They've got a light and lovely
Cheval Blanc. I suppose it won't give you asthma…

Genesis

Bit by bit
we eat into an island
of associations.

Like mad, we say.
We eat madly.
The island will never be the same again.

That forest
is the colour of sweet pickle,
those sand dunes
no more than dignified potato chips.

And what is the sea about them
but water plus a little salt,
plankton-tabasco and deep blue
vegetable colouring?

Suppose dark matter
reconstituted water.
Lightning might strike again
and ergo life.

Or life in another
dimension of time
with poets, priests, physicists
supping together.

This is the way
we underwrite our world
and try to contain it.

This is the red lane
our minds slide down.

A Kensington Vespers

(i)

There are no words
in the afterlife;
a sound reason
to have nothing to do with it.

But if, when we die,
we re-join our dead
mothers and fathers,
and old forebear Darwin,

how full of noises
will the island be: how lively
the songs, arguments, shrieking;

thunder, sea chewing loud
on its own margin,
high wind or Zephyr's
benign one a background

music for young women
laughing at a picnic in sunshine
or the pop of a cork,

gurgle of Fleurie
cooled by a spring until
poured into a cup; what utterance,

what birdsong from past
time to lull us through eternity,
warmed by a sun not burning to death
but spiralling back to be reborn.

In the beginning, the word
said John, the loved one.
We become archaeologists
of evening. We resurrect a buried day.

(ii)

A friend in advertising
    said that Lux
Eternum – sic – was the name
    of a discarded
lotion: the idea being
to wash yourself with it,
    then shampoo
your youthful, revitalised,
    cascading hair.

(iii)

There are worse places to dip your toe
in Lethe than the Serpentine in November.
Beech turned russet gold against a grey
raincloud over the City, with light wind
planes dump leaves like devalued money
or a benediction. There is time to walk
west down Kensington High and disappear
into the sun's throat. Barker's behind you,
built in the decade when you were born,
you fear no evil; all the crowds and cars
are moving quite slowly: horses of night.
The Odeon cinema features everyone's life
on multiple screens; you just sneak on by
for shelter among Blue Plaque memorials:
Chesterton, Frankie Howerd – neighbours
visited via *Thursday*, *Lepanto*, *Up Pompeii*.
You hear them calling, and a childhood calling.
The going down of the sun is swifter now
than jets descending patiently for Heathrow;
marine life, inverted. The outer marker
is almost visible. Worse days to go to ground.

Of Paradise

Montale's sad, tail-coated waiter
muttered, 'No-one orders sweet wines now'
but at this end of town everyone knows
it's eating foie gras to the sound of trumpets.
At home in Wales, on a given Easter Sunday,
freed from all the pent-up irritation
at the C of W mangling the Liturgy,
we feast, one day a year, on apocalyptically
expensive first-run salmon; our Easter eggs
transformed into celestial hollandaise.
Steadying, still, to study the Smith of Smiths'
advice to a young lady in depression:
keep good blazing fires; be firm and constant
in the exercise of rational religion.
Eliot handled Russell and Wittgenstein
by seeing off such a contradiction in terms
with foresight, because, in his lifetime,
physicists turn time upside down,
biochemists find its blueprint in the veins
of everyone...

        For Eliot, where people prayed
intently, prayer was valid; the place holy;
answers irrelevant, being of the future.
Dante and Dodgson sought intermediation
for the love that moves the sun and other stars
through the clear gaze of a pubescent girl.
St Auden, although resolutely queer
(he loathed all suggestion of gaiety),
found, in an *Alice* essay, that humankind
seldom lofts higher than a twelve-year-old
intelligent female.

        To most of us, heaven is childhood.
Wordsworth goes further and locates it in infancy.
Ethics are negative: don't be vile to each other;
ease any pain you can, wherever you sense it;
leave resurrection to the mathematicians.
Look back. Your future's behind you. QED's
no longer Latin for *Sod off* or *So there*
but quantum electrodynamics, a love-child
of Mr Magnetic Force and Ms Relativity.

At home, the paradisal is vegetative:
scabbard reeds, broken light by the river Shannon;
Mediterranean flash of blue through olive trees;
bay boletus in a dense dark wood in Wales.
Time's physical and therefore temporal.
There was beginning, there will be some end of time.
One firework fizzles then lets loose a second one.

Primavera for Pembroke Gardens

(i)

Sad spring: already trees
begin to lose definition.
From outer and higher branches
a green adolescent fuzz
creeps over them.

Knicker-pink cherry blossom
blunts laurel blades
at the side of the house to rhyme,
badly, with brake lights

and the last Belisha beacon
in W8 beyond. Today traffic,
lighter than usual, is still intrusive.
Roadworks resurrect the First World War.
Security alarms are perky,

seem to be ringing all over the Royal
Borough.
       Noise, unease,
but a rumour of wild life
getting on with stuff in the nervous light
of early evening. Our local vixen
is rearing her cubs in a deep declivity
behind rubbery dustbins. She has drawn blank

in the big gardens, grandiloquent mansions
of overseas owners: the sad, patrolled,
stucco bolt-holes of an Arab, Russian,
occasional indigenous plutocracy

tweeting its money to the Cayman Islands
and thence to Savill, Chesterton, Knight Frank.
Vacant homes have few leavings. Fox
will dance over the wall for nearby Waitrose
waste. One night she worried a yoghurt carton
to drag it spilled and heavy to the cubs.
Clever. Last year the borough council

smoked out wasps who constructed
their Frank Gehry nest in the shower vent
of our bathroom. Now a pair of blue
tits have taken a shine to the oversized
satellite dish up-ended on next door's chimney
which rises from an investment, not a dwelling.

(ii)

Sad spring but doolally days
of summer are coming in, engines
of life beginning to tick over.
Soon contractors will open dead mansions,
whisk away dustsheets, fill vases up
with tulips and orchids. The Gulf is warming
as emirs stir for the annual pilgrimage
to Kensington and Knightsbridge.
                              Lambos, Ferraris
crated up for the visit, air-freighted
here and back again, make a carbon feast

for Whitsun but for us, the indigènes,
what future? This part of London,
haunt, years back, of uncles and grandmothers,
is gift-wrapped also, sent from another planet.
Foxes are fun but we miss humanity
cheek by jowl and breathing in Chiswick, Brixton;
all the humane postcodes and busy boroughs,
not these hedged-off, silent catacombs.

It is Jubilee year, the diamond.
Our sovereign, Commonwealth-minded, colour-blind,
is governor still of the Church of England's
worldwide Anglican episcopate.
Her relatives dwell in stalls, just up the road.
May she bring off the Derby before she goes.

On TV an Asiatic weather lady
smiles encouragement from her isobars.
The old men plan a walk through Barnes wetlands
and then lunch: today's pasta and Sangiovese.
Romans came first round here, at least where city
swivels towards the Thames to search for sea.

Henry was hunting at Richmond when they severed
Boleyn's little neck and sent him a smoke signal.
It blew over roof and field, across the river;
from a clearing you can still spot Tower Hill.
We have reached the age of burning love letters.
Who wants old endearments notarised?
Lament, if you can, if only for a moment,
Fletchers, Hodgsons: lost maternal Kensington;
cricketing, upright, English bourgeoisie
now dwindled like the Early Service attendance
at St Mary Abbots. Lives waver. Other lives.

Winter Song

for my brother

A dying shame:
no longer here
to pick our season.

Kensington June: the stucco
wastes, the rich green.
Good to escape

for our old imagined
late 19th-century
post–train, pre–car
Mediterranean

where sun and wine
come cheap
and flesh warm.

Good to fly
where night drops
like lead each evening,
fishermen strike flares

and the round sun slides,
behind Gibraltar,
back into the grey
embrace of our childhood's

immeasurable Atlantic.
Spring, 'with its spirit
of divine discontent and longing',
may turn the tide, autumn

augment a belief
in self, maturity:
myths, like the gods,
but natural.

If we could choose,
we'd sweep everything away
and head for winter,

our eyes open
to the skeletal grace
of leafless trees.

V

Nursery Rhyme for Ninety

Occasional Verses

Nursery Rhyme for Ninety

for Brian Urquhart

Apricot apple
blueberry bun;
coffee with everything,
fumbles and fun.

O bright summer day!
Perfectible night!
The Shakers are shaking.
The Berkshires are bright.

At ninety each summer's
a bunch, a reward
for an unsentimental
guy who's worked hard

to stop our poor species'
balloon going up;
the filth on the fan
another failed crop

of decisions affecting
the poor of the earth
who turn to Manhattan
in fury and faith

there might be some other,
just one or two,
disinterested, dogged
persons like you

to point out the obvious:
killing won't work.
A snake eats the dust but
a hydra bites back.

Close to your home
it took barely an hour
to fling hunger's bowl
against luxury's tower.

We shall be sweeping
the debris away
for how long? A generation? Two?
You won't say

but pick yourself up,
get on with your jobs:
point out the obvious,
save us from Hobbes.

Your life has been lovely,
humane and long.
Clear sight can be painful.
You wish you'd been wrong

about Arnhem, the bridge
that proved much too far
or when Congo felled Dag
or today: Gaza.

Rumour goes you escaped
an African noose
by persuading your captors
it wasn't much use

from their point of view
to put you away:
create needless trouble
in the UN, USA;

cause interruption
of precious supply.
You seemed too sensible,
not too frightened, to die.

Scottish Enlightenment
come down to earth
and Christ do we need it!
The small, blatant truth

that enough is a feast,
Creation is fine
and *I'll look after yours*
if you look after mine.

Dear Brian, I wish you
at least a decade
to chivvy, to show us
how order is made

from sense and a little
imaginative awe.
If we threaten Creation
she will show us the door.

I cannot imagine
the *New York Review*
with no (mildly) exasperated
essay by you

to ground us and keep our
feet on the ground
or the Empire State Building
with no you around

or wind through the cornfields
below Tyringham
or snow on your birthday
yielding to sun

with meltwater droplets
making their way
across the Atlantic
towards Neiti and Grey

like beads in the Bolly
we are raising to you
and Sydney and Charlie
and Rachel, and a few

good men and women
who care for this small,
Googleable, fragile,
space cannonball,

who praise you for being
and find you a star.
My dear chap, that's excessive.
Indeed. But you are.

A bright one. Immortal
through what you have done.
Applejuice, applejack,
feasting and fun,

jumpjockey figure
with lopsided smile
and a genius for making
our lives here worthwhile

a little while longer.
Predictable night,
before you enfold us
give us some light

to look our existence
clear in the eye.
Cream in our coffee.
Blueberry pie.

Sir Brian Urquhart was born on 28 February 1919. As a young major in Intelligence in the Second World War, he warned that Operation Market Garden would fail. After the war he was one of the architects of the UN and rose to be Assistant Secretary-General. In the early 1960s the UN sent him to Congo. He is a biographer of Dag Hammarskjöld.

Four Eight Two Thousand

Our long northern summer light is predictable
only for unpredictability.
Wild winds from Orkney, mist on the Wash, a flood tide
off the Cinque Ports or Thamesmouth playing tag with man's
intentions cancel parties and picnics and plans.
Yet weather does not faze Your Majesty.

You make a weather for your friends to share:
a microclimate of music, feasting and fun
with talk of tomorrow as if it were today
or yesterday, because all the people are there
in everything said: a kingdom of everyone.

To us, to millions this August is especial.
Do you care for birthdays, who makes a birthday from
each day the Almighty or the bright sun ordains?
No word when a plethora of cheering
crowds all the mails and florists, the untold
names – the occasion rarer than pale Welsh gold,
undevalued, undevaluable:
bracelets of rainbow sunshine when it rains.

Now you work all day long at celebration;
Queen and Empress the year that I was born,
Lady Elizabeth Coeur-de-Lion
always. Your heartbeat was ours in the fearsome years.
Sharing its suffering and defying its tears,
you are our island's story, our Shakespeare play.
Let us give back a little, this one birthday.

May good Scots salmon silver-gleam for you
who knows more about England than England knows
these iconoclastic days; may the wizened oaks
of the last millennium smile in the Great Park
and thrushes stage fly-pasts at Royal Lodge
and narcissi rise again, unseasonably,
chafing the rhododendrons; may the Norfolk bees
double their honeyed efforts, roses flame
like Ascot colours; may all good things stay the same
and may we remain true as you are true.

Miss Otis really regrets that she is unable
to dine with you on your birthday today,
Madam. All the rest of us at the table,
whosoever we are, wherever we may be,
will raise a glass to grant you life and laughter
for bringing light to our dark century.

Letter to James Tate

A bucket of old airs, broken graces
bangs in my head and will spill dangerously
over the temple if I am not careful.
Hung, surreptitious, I scan the thing
and discover (Joy = James) that inside
there are songs – most of them by you.
Thursday's looking up. I plan a lunch
you'd like: a TV-dinner cornucopia.
There may be trouble with the invitations.

Then the Atlantic's wild but after some
tunes I fool it into becoming a table.
You sit the American end with lots of room
for manoeuvre. Ravenous Venetians
crowd into Galway and cause misunderstanding.
'You've got the imagination of your face,'
you tell me –
tolerance deepening our conceit.

Later I learn you will be flying mid-
west for a time to finalise someone
nearer to you than sounds.
Your peace and safety are important
as anything, even our future meeting.
At thirty I eye the future like a woman
eyeing a man she might mistake for me.

Whatever the world is, it is open.
No one will be lost who finds love
in the void. People drink your health,
frosting their glasses, James, in January,
each clink welcome as music. My day
turns off before yours, thankful that
even the mild pilot who cuts his jet
over Kansas is there to steer you home by stars.

The Bidden Guest

for Vivien Duffield

When 'Omer smote 'is bloomin' lyre
Sea Goddess II was not for hire
And Vivien's birthday cruise a thought
To no fleece-haunted Argonaut,
The wine-dark seas untrodden on
By *Metcalfe* or *Mavroleon*;
Ithaca's sad Penelope
Never had the chance to see
The beauty of *Judy Taubman* shopping
Nor hear the corks of Clicquot popping
And at her loom would seek relief
Unsubcontracted by *Lord Sieff*;
Nor did the aged bard record
Events on film, like *Kathy Ford.**
Even that most august of pens
Might quail before *Lord Lichfield*'s lens
Or *Hedgecoe*'s; why, he never saw
Fiona Allsopp pining for
Her trip into the wild blue yonder,
Mistaking Henries *Ford* for *Fonda*,
Nor longed to touch each well-stocked sari
Of the wife (and her sister) of *Philip Harari* –
Unless those tales about Greeks are true
In which case he'd long for you know who.
Bereft of sleep on the ocean wave,
I summon him from beyond the grave
To join us; he would find, I'm sure,
Our Odyssey worth waiting for
And once the awful shocks were past,
The whole trip a terrific blast
And what's more, quite familiar.
Aliai Forte is Nausicaa
In anyone's language: even Homer
Would be guilty of a misnomer
Not to see that, though I suppose
Theresa Sackler runs her close.

* *Cruise One alone (alas) I sing:*
Cruise Two was spared this kind of thing.

Vivien is Circe, for her gen-
Erosity makes pigs of men –
And women (I must say you could fool
Me, looking at most of them round the pool).
Jackie Stewart's is a trade
(Or art) from which our myths are made
And as for heroes, *Jocelyn* will
(With *Roger Moore*) quite fit the bill
Unless you like a hairy chest:
Then *Harry Fitzgibbons* would be best.
Of sirens I fear I must confess
We have an *embarras de richesses*
And knowing what is good for me,
Refuse to name one, or two, or three
(Decent, I feel, because the thing is
My wife has a thing for *Johnny Menzies*).
You can spot them by the way they swoon
To the slinky songs of *Eck McEwen*.
The dear old boy would like the grub
And even share a Jacuzzi tub
With *Sherwood* or *George Weidenfeld*
Given th'esteem in which both are held
(One bidding for his memoirs, t'other
Saving the Greeks a lot of bother
By shipping the Trojans and their retainers
En masse to Venice in containers).
If he fell into a pet he'-
D lull to the songs of *Gordon Getty*;
Gasp at *Olga Polizzi*'s stories
Of goings-on among the Tories;
Engage in some engaging shilly-
Shally with *Maureen*, wife of *Billy*;
Listen to *Sarah Hogg* or eat a
Lobster with *Sunny* and *Rosita*
And keep himself from having fits
By gazing at *Rocco Forte*'s tits,
For when the Ancients' spirits sag
They brood on the British taste for drag
(A fetish that forms no part of the bond,
Thank God, between *Mr* and *Mrs Blond*
And is not known to be a vice
Of *Charlie* or of *Carol Price*).
With *Gowrie* and *Allsopp* here to sell
Him art, *Tom Parr* and *Amabel*

(Or *Tessa*, to hell with the expense)
Tarting his cabin up with chintz
Supplied at cost by *Lady Jane*
There'd be enough to ease the pain
Of having tri-millennial bones
Or listening to *Rhydian Morgan-Jones*,
Not least with his royalties in the care
Of *Edgar de P.* or *Jacob R.*
(Good news, that is, if he were able
To keep them from *Benson* at the table).
By *Ritblat* housed, by *Weinberg* covered,
He would forget he'd ever suffered
And joining us all in the applause,
Forsake dark deeds and tales of wars,
Fulfil at last the wish of men
(His Muse for ever *Vivien*),
Leave epic to the gods above
And write, like me, with thanks and love.

Bread-and-Butter Letter

We sailed from Barcelona
to the port of mayonnaise
and drifted through an island
paradise of days.

We climbed the fort of Figeac
by the bay of Beychevelle
and louder grew our voices
with taller tales to tell.

The sea was calm at dinner;
no one made a mess.
The sun was always golden,
like a saffron bouillabaisse.

Schoenberg and Strauss regaled us.
Picasso came to draw
a picture of a bullshot:
a legless toreador.

We planned an exhibition of
Uccello in Berlin.
All the crew were handed
a miniature of gin.

The old town of Skorthalia
gleamed from its shining hill.
If you breathe in deeply
you can breathe it still.

Soon we shall have to travel
north and meet our fate;
our hearts in love, our bodies
a trifle overweight.

But ever to the rescue
rides memory: relief
in the form of a fine risotto,
a sharp balsamic beef

and it is almost wasteful
critically to speak
of that *fritture* of calamaris:
a masterpiece, in Greek.

Mahler indeed is moving.
His music can bring tears.
But so, in recollection,
does the *tarte Tatin* of pears.

Goddess, Astarte, bring us
blessings while we gorge.
Grant us the perfect figure of
Maria and of George.

(What wicked, Faustian
bargain have they struck?
Is it their generous nature?
Is it genes? Or luck?)

Banish pride within us
and envy, the curse of men,
but let us at least be greedy
enough to come again

and climb Rock Candy Mountain
and sail the seven seas
of Pomerol and Pauillac
and other luxuries.

Because through gleams of splendour
an appetite for life
is forged. It helps protect us.
There will be time for strife.

Blessings on George, Maria;
bring them safe to shore;
set their dreams to music plus
a thunderous encore

and if, as it is rumoured,
you need a sacrifice,
Astarte (eating children
is not very nice),

accept, as you survey your
creatures from above,
this trifling canapé of
gratitude and love.

Clerihew

The Viking
was never greatly to my liking.
To him, village
rhymed with pillage;

yet I have to confess,
under some duress,
occasionally I feel torn
for he founded the jaunty city of Dublin
                          where I was born.

Ballade Tragique

Poor old Lord Golly is looking quite sick.
His sponsoring Minister's giving him stick.
Her name is Virginia, a good-looking lass,
But she thinks the Arts Council's a pain in the elbow
(Which is only poetic justice, you see,
For her proper name is Ms Bolmondely).
It isn't her duties that she's prone to shirk,
Though she'd rather be photographed working than work,
But the rushing about like a hen with no neck
Is making his lordship's existence a wreck
(He mumbles at meetings; he chokes on his tea;
He thinks that the Shadow is still Jenny Lee).
The Arts Council comes last, the Tourist Board first –
As if Rachel Whiteread were Damien Hirst.
She thinks that the tourists come from overseas
To gaze open-mouthed at our bureaucracies
And though more than sixty thousand she's paid,
She confuses the Lottery loot with Grant Aid.
DNH, on the whole an indifferent bunch
(Nick Kroll and Melanie aren't out to lunch),
Connive at these follies; their folly-*bergère*
Will keep quiet so long as the cameras are there.
The Permanent Sec does not give a stuff
('That floppy-tied fellow's had more than enough')
For he knows that by keeping his eye on the ball
The new British Library won't open at all
And if four hundred million has gone down the drain,
The taxpayer will not be bothered again.
Now that he's sure he's all things to all men
The Treasury beckons – 'Dare I say Number Ten?' –
And 'All that you need to handle our Ginny
Is to think of her baking a cake in her pinny.
The Lotto, she tells me, is "utterly brill"
And if the Arts Council "goes down a few mill",
She says, "When I count all the buildings I've given,
They should feel that they've died and gone straight up to heaven.
Haydn, is it like Grey to be such a defeatist?
I'm afraid that at bottom he's just an elitist
Who thinks that the opera and ballet and all
Count for more than brass bands or community hall-

S in Scunthorpe or Woking: it's *so* out of touch
To fuss about Schubert and Shakespeare and such
Or Beckett or Pinter… Good grief! It's not wrong
To want to give people a knees-up, a song,
A night on the tiles: they've earned it, God knows,
And they don't want a treat like *The Name of the Rose*
Set to music by Birtwistle… You can't take your aunt
To most of the plays with an Arts Council grant.
Then nude males all over the Royal Festival Hall –
What on earth must Her Majesty make of it all?
I'm a tolerant woman, my best friends are gay
But they don't put their thingies on public display.
That Mapplethorpe, really!
                                    You know I'm no prude
But even dear Peter finds fist-fumbling rude
If you'll pardon my French… What's he up to? Lord G,
Not Peter, I mean. He's out to get me!
He knows, I suspect, that while I'm no coward
I can't face that look in the eye from Mike Howard
Much longer: *he* wants everything banned,
Artists slung into gaol: then where will *I* stand?
Oh golly! I tell you, I miss my last slot.
Closing wards is a doddle compared to this lot.
Haydn, will Grey be an absolute beast
And make theatres go dark in the South and South East
Before May? He's gone native; he can't be a Tory;
He's only concerned with his personal glory
Not mine."
                    She fetchingly pouts. "Well, we shall see.
I'm prettier, nicer, more caring than he.
And at least I'll say this for my Shadow, and Blair,
They've rumbled m'lord, an hereditary peer,
Who's deserted his faith and will not cross swords
With Labour to cling to his seat in the Lords."

So she witters until I uncork my Welsh smile
In order to make her belt up for a while.
"I must keep off politics, Secretary of State,
But I know what a lot I've heaped on your plate
Just lately, and if I may speak as a chum –
Please don't drop me in it, be sure to keep mum –
These matters are on *my* mind too, night and day,
And while there's a great deal in all that you say,
The Budget's too close now, not much can be done.

Still, the battle's not lost till the battle is won
And I promise I'll have a word in the ear
Of Sir Terry; you settle the hash of that peer."
And then I'll be certain to see out my days
As Sir *Haydn, not* Mr *Facing-Both-Ways.*'

Prince, Goddess, Apollo, Artemis descend
And rescue Lord Golly, the Muses' one friend!
They answer. The worm turns. With hideous glee,
He lets loose the last handguns at his Ministry.
Now he's deep in a cell for the evil insane
BUT
        THE CULTURE
                OF ENGLAND
                        IS SAFE
                                ONCE AGAIN.

A Cannelopouliad

Dear Angelos, three score years and ten!
Do boys at last turn into men?
I hope not, if by men we mean
World-weary fellows, epicene
Cynics who have seen it all;
Grandees too grand to return your call
Themselves, but have 'their people' do it;
Know-nothings who never really knew it;
Tough eggs with fragile egos; chaps
With teeth as white as yachting caps
And his'n'hers Ferraris; guys
Who judge a painting by the price
It makes at auction; blokes, in short,
We'd rather leave behind in port
And would not welcome to your party
At Vouliagmeni or on *Astarte*.

Dear Friend, we beg you not to grow
Up too quickly: your *putto*
Mischievous smile, your *Bengel* jokes
Remind me of Hermes, god who pokes
Fun at the gods and gets away
With it to laugh another day.
Plato, of course, is looking pained
But Plato needs your jokes explained
To him and – don't it make you sick? –
The guy banned poets from his Republic.
Forgeddabadim. Your logos
Appeared to me on Mykonos
Or was it St Petersburg? New York?
Or over a truffled *pied-de-porc*
In Koffmann's caff (it's called *Tante Claire*;
I'd like to spend my old age there)?
Wherever it was, we found our lives
Entwined. Our flawless German wives
Are fond of us (and to each other
Sisters – what's the Greek for brother?)
At least in English: when they natter
In *Deutsch* it's quite another matter.
Though I may doubt that you'll believe

A Brit with his heart worn on his sleeve,
I've got to say – aw shucks, oh screw
It all – I'm blessed with a pal like you.

But what to give you, a clever gent
Who made his mountain in cement
And has the manners not to care
If you are a fellow squillionaire
Or not? A case of Krug? Beluga?
A Brigitte Bardot doll in nougat?
A ring for navel, nose or ear
As worn by many a British peer?
A couple of Mr Purdey's guns?
A Dictionary of Dreadful Puns?
(Now there's a thought.) A perpetual cask
Of Chivas Regal? Only ask,
Dear Angelos, and we will try:
The only limit is the sky.
Never will you be short-changed.
The mortgage finance is arranged.

What's this you tell us? 'Just drop by
Vouliagmeni in July.
I need no gew-gaws for my shelves.
My birthday present is yourselves.'

Typical Cannelopoulos
Kindness that almost makes us cross.
When I faced my Thermopylae
I sent for the Cannelopouli.
We want to do a little better
Than that so I send this rhyming letter
(Homer nodded, don't forget)
And pray that Zeus will weave his net
Loosely for you, that Aphrodite
Continue paying rent to Heide,
Hermes lend us wings to fly
Safely to Athens by and by,
Even Poseidon aim to please
With balmy airs and gentle seas,
Dionysius turn on the juice,
With here *La Tâche* and there *Pétrus*,
While high Parnassus Muses sing
An anthem to their Angel king.

Mere mortals we, with whom gods play,
May hold our heads up high to say
Evcharistó for your birthday
And XXX, Neiti and Grey.

A Refusal

Down her stairs in a diamond tiara
swept the Countess of March and Kinrara
and no dress at all
so the Great Goodwood Ball
was much missed by her ancient admirer.

An Horatian Ode on the Visit of Lucy Ann Josephine Butler Sloss (aet. m. vii) to her Grandparents, John and Anya Sainsbury, Residing at Aghios Stephanos, Corfu, and Accompanied by her Parents, Bobby and Sarah Butler Sloss, during August MCMXCVI

(i)

Lucy Ann Josephine Butler Sloss
Her sea-green eyes and her hair like moss;
I shall propose as soon as poss
To Lucy Ann Josephine.

(ii)

Lucy Ann Josephine Butler Sloss
At home on Corfu or the island of Cos;
I must save up and buy her a *Schloss*;
Lucy Ann Josephine.

(iii)

Lucy Ann Josephine Butler Sloss
Laughs when her teaspoons skittle across
The marble floor – it is hard to get cross
With Lucy Ann Josephine.

(iv)

When I voice misgivings about the EU,
She murmurs a soft and sceptical 'Coo'.
Helmut Kohl is no match for you,
Lucy Ann Josephine.

Tiberius' pool has no fears for her.
All the house party cares for her.
Lizards remain in their lairs for her,
Lucy Ann Josephine.

(vi)

Alas by the time she is twenty-one
My sun will be set, my day nearly done,
Though faint heart never fair lady won,
Lucy Ann Josephine.

(vii)

What will you care for my ancient name,
My magnificent profile, my wealth and fame
When I totter about on my Zimmer frame,
Lucy Ann Josephine?

(viii)

When she smiles such selfish desires
Blow themselves out like forest fires.
I truly wish her a chap she admires,
Lucy Ann Josephine.

(ix)

Meanwhile there is plenty of stuff to be done:
Morals, exams, battles lost and won.
Learning your life is not always fun,
Lucy Ann Josephine.

May you attach, with God's good grace,
Your own good mind to your own fair face.
Your father gives you an edge in that race,
Lucy Ann Josephine.

Your mother will teach you to cherish books
And walk by the Thames and talk to the ducks.
– Unfair if you also inherit her looks,
Lucy Ann Josephine.

And both your parents are mad about you,
And think up amusing things to do
And even keep calm when you go to the loo,
Lucy Ann Josephine.

If you gave me a magic wand,
I'd wish you your Grandpa's power to command
And still be kind to all in our land,
Lucy Ann Josephine;

Your grandmother's all-seeing clarity,
Who dances on life like sun on the sea
Unlike clod-hopping old coves like me,
Lucy Ann Josephine.

(xv)

Lucy Ann Josephine Butler Sloss,
The Millennium's gain is the Century's loss.
So turn your back on all that is dross,
Lucy Ann Josephine,

(xvi)

And in our hearts, be they old or young,
As poets ancient and modern have sung,
You, who already have climbed the first rung,
Will reign forever as Queen.

Birthday Card for Francesca von Habsburg

Darling Chessie, may your day
of birth be one long rondelay
of all that Austria has grown
from *Schlag* and *Schmaltz* to the twelve-tone
crew like dear old Schoen- and Berg
or Webern, whom I find no *Zwerg*.
Here in our misty northern isle
you're loved in every stately pile.
Even the most moth-eaten peer
would take you to *Rosenkavalier*.
We fancy you down to your socks.
You treat us just like Baron Ochs.
Your mother gave you sense and beauty;
your father your aesthetic duty
to do the best you can to save
man's artefacts from the usual grave
of exploitation or neglect.
Love's wedded, therefore, to respect.
Your husband and your children are
blessed by an effervescent star
that fizzles and I'm game to bet
is years from fizzling out just yet.
Forty, you'll find, will come to be
like bathing in our own North Sea:
wonderful, once you are in.
Just keep your distance from the gin.
But on this day, oh heart's dear daughter,
all is forgiven: *Sachertorte*
(best made with almonds), *Schnitzels*, *Schnapps*…
May the sun shine and no mishaps
or guestly boorishnesses mar
the birth of such a superstar.
May your dress outrival Klimt,
may neighbours not be *unbestimmt*,
may wild boars in the forests listen
and all the *Vögelein* feathers glisten
and please, just for a second, spare
a thought for one who can't be there
but will in his northern fastness pray
for your life and happiness. Love from Grey.

Portrait of the Writer as a Regency Rector

Of Derry (in dreams) and Raphoe
he was Bishop. With money to blow
he kept a fine table
and an excellent stable
of hunters with plenty of go.

His sermons were witty and short,
his cellar renowned for its port.
For a foretaste of heaven
just try the '07.
He protected his parish from Thought.

A Trinity man, he'd been told
to believe that the glitter was gold,
to be kind to the poor
(he employed twenty-four)
and bring buckets of soup to the old.

He was pipped, through treacherous Deans,
by a parson called Farster, from Queen's,
with a grim view of life,
scruffy children, a wife
named Mavis without any means.

The faithful dwindled, unchoired.
Enthusiasts flourished, inspired
by the endless revisions,
doctrinal divisions…
He abandoned all hope and expired.

Our Deity's puzzling: He grieves
for scholars and paupers and thieves.
You meet sportsmen and peers
with that fellow downstairs,
not people one seldom receives.

And yet it may not be so odd.
Old Berkeley was right about God
and the curious ways
of the Ancient of Days.
Soon we'll be under the sod.

Bellocian Border Ballad

for Marcus Clements

When the Duke of Buccleuch
got locked in the leuch
of a pub at Renfrew
people hadn't a cleuch.

He was locked in all day
and his gentle 'I say!',
his 'Is anyone there?'
was ignored by a crowd
that was drinking, and loud,
but at last caught the ear,
of Lord Golly, a peer
much lower in rank
and with less in the bank,
but kind.
        He, appalled,
downed his pint and then called
the local police
who ensured the release
by smearing some grease
on the key…

The Duke smiled his charming,
forgiving, disarming,
munificent, calming
smile and just muttered 'Whoopee.'
He stood everyone drinks
and a round on the links
(quite easy, because he owned three).

There was joy in Dalkeith
and wee girls wove a wreath
for his brow.

The good folk of Selkirk
got two days off work;
the Chief of Police
the Freedom of Dumfries
and they even made merry

in the street of Queensberry
while refusing to make too much row.

For the Dukes of Buccleuch
always know what to deuch
like the Lords Montageuch
and the Scotts
(though I fear I must pass
by the clan of Douglas;
there is always one apple that rots
in the barrel).
                          His Grace
can now show his face
all over Scotland,
not just that province of Goth-land
to the south.

He may now reassume
the sceptre, the plume
and his rights to Bowhill.
Bad winds that blow ill
have been driven away
by the Ruthvens – hooray! –
and no one is down in the mouth.

So three cheers for a chap
who can take a mishap
on the chin.
Three cheers for a duke
much too kind to rebuke
the incompetent trog
who left him in the bog
bolted in…

Ah the Dukes of Buccleuch
always know what to deuch
and that is why yeuch
and I should admire 'em
and why they survive
and continue to thrive.
Three beuchs for all folk who'd retire 'em.

Lament

Then there's old Golly, one of the sweetest
but altogether an elitist.
Anything to do with soccer
quickly drives him off his rocker.
He'd rather have you break his thumbs
than contemplate the muddy bums
(male ones, too) in Rugby League.
Cricket induces mild fatigue.
He is not prone to go on benders,
has never taken in *EastEnders*
and as for down the pub, I fear
claret's his thing, not lager beer.
If you want to catch him you'll need to loiter
near the Wigmore Hall. A confirmed Bayreuther,
he's sat through the sixteen hours of *The Ring*
nine times and clapped like anything.
He drives a seven-year-old car
but his audio cost more than a Jaguar.
He never goes tie-less and I suspec-
t clubbing means White's, not discotheque.
He complains, when I drop by for tea,
of the dumbing-down of Radio Three.
Bartok's quartets and those of Brahms
welcome his ears with open arms
and when his spirit needs a boost
he spends a night or two with Proust.
Cool, to him, means finding art in
Jean-Baptiste Chardin and Agnes Martin.
In politics he thinks it lax
to spend more than you take in tax.
He's Tory, High Church C of E.
I don't think he's the chap for me
but this I'll give him, this I'll say:
he noticed what I wore today.

Angela's Dream

I cannot do business with Bohrer.
I wonder if anyone can.
My Jewish friends call him a *schnorrer*.
He is a most worrying man.

He knows quite a lot about Hölder-
lin and, so people say, Kleist,
but he seems to give me the cold shoulder.
I don't think we'll ever get spliced.

My sister insists he's good-looking.
Really? He looks rather wild.
As for brains, you'd expect the top booking
from a Teuto-Hibernian child.

Will he dandle my seven grandchildren
or bury himself in Merkur?
Like Macbeth faced with wife, witch and cauldron
he has reservations, I'm sure.

I'd like to do business with Bohrer,
I admit. We shall just have to see.
To his Petrarch can I be a Laura?
Can Bohrer do business with me?

It might be quite fun to speak German
again after twenty-five years.
Shall we just have a fling or a perman-
ent thing – do I care if he cares?

Will my girlfriends call me Frau Professor?
Will I ever see London again?
Campus life's a tremendous depressor
and Stanford's twelve hours in a plane.

Good grief, I've just woken beside him.
I am faced with a fait accompli
and find that I've gone and allied him
and Bohrer's done business with me.

VI

Memoir

Remembering Robert Lowell

A few days before he died in September 1977, Robert Lowell told me: 'When I die, Elizabeth's shares will rise and mine will fall.' This proved prophetic. Elizabeth Bishop is a pure poet, each poem its own subject and first cause. Lowell is a poet haunted by and trying to accommodate history. He is an allusive writer for contemporary tastes, classically educated and steeped in European as well as American literature. He was a Winslow as well as a Lowell. His forebears helped to establish America. Even his most autobiographical poems show a figure in an historical landscape, bounded and buffeted by events. That September evening in County Kildare he added: 'My shares will come back.' He was revisiting his third wife and Muse, the Dolphin of his later poems. This was the Irish writer Caroline Blackwood. Months earlier he had left her to live again with another wonderful writer, his second wife Elizabeth (Lizzie) Hardwick. The story informs his last book, *Day by Day*. A few days later he flew to New York carrying a Lucian Freud portrait of Caroline, married to Freud in the early 1950s, which I had procured for him. He died in the cab going home to Lizzie, the Dolphin's picture on his lap. He was sixty.

What kind of person made the poems and letters? All you need do is read them to find out. He was not in the least narcissistic and was able to cast a cold eye on his own troubles and condition, a sympathetic one on other people's. He was an enchanting man. The Ian Hamilton biography is well sourced and scrupulous and Ian knew Lowell well. But he brought too many of his own personal and poetic preconceptions to the portrait. 'Reading Ian,' Lizzie told me, 'you'd never know why we all loved Cal so much.' In the unfair way of life, Cal was very good-looking.

When I first met Lowell in the mid-1960s, I was determined not to fall under his spell. I had been knocking about with American poets who disapproved deeply of his work: Charles Olson, John Wieners, Robert Creeley and other disciples of Olson, with whom I had shared an apartment for a couple of months. This was a re-run of the old row between the American avant garde and T.S. Eliot: he deserted us; his work was too polite, too British, too referential. But when I arrived at Harvard I did want to take Lowell's poetry course. You had to submit poems; dozens did so; you were lucky to get in. Course members would tear each other's poems to bits under his gleeful direction. But if – and this was always a bit hit or miss – he truly liked a poem, nothing was too good for you. He'd get your number, ring you up, tell you to call him 'Cal' and invite you to lunch. He'd even bully editors to publish your work. Most of the class made a name for themselves.

In a way unconnected to his looks or his fame, Lowell was terrific company. He had a giant frame of reference, the whole of Western history and literature, and he enjoyed locating even his most ordinary friends and acquaintances within this frame. He also liked teasing – how different from powerful Olson or deliberative Creeley. He thought the fact that a British lord had fallen in with Black Mountain poets the funniest thing he had heard in years. He also teased me for telling the class that the best young poets lived in Belfast. I got the last laugh here as he came to revere Seamus Heaney and see the point of my own equal admiration for Michael Longley and Derek Mahon.

I became Lowell's teaching assistant, gofer and companion when he was ill. My first wife and I, and our child and our dog, gave him something of a second home in Cambridge; Lizzie and he shared magnificent apartments in New York as well as the house in Castine which he describes in 'Fourth of July in Maine'. He was what is nowadays called bipolar. He would write when depressed; then the writing would cheer him up; then he'd become funny and cocky and sociable; then he'd fall clunkingly, and often unsuitably, in love; then the mixture of excitement and guilt – he was devoted to Lizzie and Harriet – would point him towards the bin. I still believe, over forty years on now, that I could find my way from Appleton Street in Cambridge to McLean's hospital in my sleep. Even ill, even as his speech and appearance coarsened through drugs and he wrote poems too bad to be considered for his own seminar, he kept some of his humour and grace. 'Now you *know* I'm crazy,' he said one afternoon at McLean's as, horrified, I watched him spoon thick institutional gravy over his ice cream before wolfing it down.

Cal was an unusually affectionate man and really loved his friends. In the spring of 1968 I decided to leave America. We had an emotional parting, with tears. I did not expect to see him again, or only rarely. But – nothing to do with me – he fell in love with another close friend, Caroline. They married and settled in Kent. In their early months as a couple I spent most of my time with them and then withdrew a little; I had a new life of my own. Ian Hamilton, Jonathan Raban and Jonathan Miller, who had directed Cal's plays, were also close British friends. Raban has written better on Lowell than anyone, I believe. Miller does a wonderful imitation of him talking and waving his arms about: 'Cal warding off ideas with his hands,' as Jonathan puts it.

One of the attractive things about Lowell was the way in which in spite of his achievement and immense body of work, he never quite grew up. He remained mischievous and a little sly – an adolescent who expected to get caught but expected, too, to be forgiven. So my own poem in his memory, 'Sisters', is prompted by that genius of adolescence, Arthur Rimbaud. Cal's version, 'The Lice Hunters', appears in *Imitations*.

When I met Lowell, he was the most renowned living poet in our language, Eliot and Auden apart. I once asked him who were his favourite modern poets. I expected him to choose Eliot, whom he loved and who was also his publisher. 'Oh, Hardy and Ezra,' he replied, 'because of the heartbreak.' Heartbreak and history. It is time to celebrate him again.

Sisters

i.m. Robert Lowell

The child, lousy, ridden with eczema
and scabrous, red and restless most of the time,
lay near an open window and tried not to itch
or fidget until the Sisters of Mercy came.

Look what happens: they sweep by on cowls
like boats to harbour from the azure blue
off Collioure; all sibilants and vowels
they set to work to make his wish come true.

Even their breathing is like the summer day,
heavy and floral, and he breathes them in
with so much longing that he starts to cry.
But then electric fingers play a tune

through thick hair to shiver inside his skull
from now on, though never better than this
morning when each skittish silver nail
tenderly crucified the little lice.

Langour and excitement alternate
within him: like Sauternes, like love affairs
he'll grow into and flee from. Sisters wait
for him to thank them, puzzled by his tears.

after Rimbaud

Notes

The following notes are designed to be useful. They are in no way essential.

The Andrians (2009)

This poem has been written for Leonidas Goulandris (1927–2009), painter and shipowner. It celebrates his work and my own friendship with him and his twin brother Alexander (Aleko). The 's' in 'Leonidas' in this poem is almost silent, so that when read aloud it often sounds like *Leoneeda*, the faint sibilant after the last syllable being voluntary and employed when it sounds appropriate. Leonidas always called me by my formal first name Alexander and never made use of my usual nickname, Grey. The poem is dedicated to Alexander Goulandris in Leonidas's memory. The Goulandris family hails from the Cycladic island of Andros.

Leonidas's work drew inspiration from the sixteenth-century hermetic philosopher Giordano Bruno (1548–1600), who was born near Naples. I am indebted to the work of the late Frances A. Yates for the quotation 'Through the light which shines…' and indeed for all references to Giordano; especially her *Giordano Bruno and the Hermetic Tradition* and *Lull and Bruno* (both Routledge and Kegan Paul).

There have been a number of studies of the so-called Gowrie Conspiracy. From the Ruthven family's perspective the conspiratorial element was a smokescreen to obscure the murder of the Earl and his brother, the Master of Ruthven. Andrew Lang, of *Red*, *Blue* etc. *Fairy Book* fame and a co-translator of Homer, published the most extensive study, *James VI and the Gowrie Mystery* (1902). William Roughead's *The Riddle of the Ruthvens* (1919), which was dedicated to Joseph Conrad, is more sympathetic to the family's view. Ruthven in this poem is pronounced *Riven*, and Killaloe in Co. Clare *Killaloo*. Plötzensee is the prison near Berlin where many of the conspirators of the 20 July 1944 attempt on Hitler's life were executed.

The terms 'harbingers' and 'forerunners' are drawn from 'The Forerunners' by George Herbert (1593–1633), the great poet born in Montgomeryshire, where I live. The reference to Wallace Stevens (1879–1955) comes from his meditative poem 'Notes Toward a

Supreme Fiction'. I am indebted for the idea, and the phrase, that the dead are 'beyond succour and hospitality' to a restaurant review in *The Sunday Times* by A.A. Gill.

The Italian Visitor (2012)

'Eastbourne'
Vince il male... 'Evil conquers... The wheel will not stop'.

'Black Trout: Reading 1948'
'of gravel and biscuitry': Reading's biggest employer was the biscuit (US cookie) factory of Huntley & Palmer, later United Biscuits.

'Argyll Tour: Glasgow 1948'
Fingal's Cave on Staffa. Although this masterpiece was bought for America directly from J.M.W. Turner's studio, British art was held in such low esteem in the mid-1950s that the Museum 'deaccessioned' it. The painting returned to England and was bought by the then Lord Astor of Hever. In the 1980s, through the agency of my then business partner, Thomas Gibson, and myself it was sold by Lord Astor to Paul Mellon. It is now back in America at the Paul Mellon Centre for British Art at Yale.

'Metropolitan Christmas 1948'
Heywood Hill is a Mayfair bookshop, founded before the war. Cinque Terre: Montale's native region of north-west Italy.

A Kensington Vespers (2012)

'Numbers'
Wisden: Wisden's Almanack, cricketing bible.

'Reece Mews'
Francis Bacon (1909–92) lived and worked at 7 Reece Mews in South Kensington from 1961 until his death in 1992. The painting described in the poem is an imaginary one, an amalgam of two late Bacon paintings. George Dyer (1934–71), a close companion of Bacon, died in a hotel in Paris during a major Bacon retrospective in the city. He is the subject of some of Bacon's greatest paintings. The Reece Mews studio has been meticulously recreated in the museum of modern art at Kilmainham in Bacon's native city of Dublin. In the 1970s I offered Dublin's Municipal Gallery an 'acceptable', i.e. clothed, full-length

portrait of Peter Lacey by Bacon. They in effect told me not to insult them.

'Reece Mews: Conversation Piece'
Miss Beeston: Valerie Beeston (1922–2005), Bacon's friend and minder at Marlborough Fine Art Ltd.
Muriel: Muriel Belcher (1908–79), militant lesbian proprietress of the Colony Club, a now defunct out-of-hours Soho drinking club frequented by Bacon and an early source of paid employment for him. One of his finest small portraits is a head of Muriel.
Israel: Israel Citkowitz (1909–74), composer and musicologist. Caroline Blackwood's second husband.
George: George Embiricos (1920–2011), Greek shipowner and art collector.
David: David Sylvester (1924–2001), writer and art critic. Close friend and champion of Bacon who introduced my wife and me to the painter in 1982.
Lucian: Lucian Freud (1922–2011), painter. Married to Caroline Blackwood in the early 1950s. She is the subject of four of his finest paintings of that period.
Caroline: Caroline Hamilton-Temple-Blackwood (1931–96), Irish writer. See also 'Memoir'.
John: John Edwards (1950–2003), friend of Francis Bacon and the painter's heir.

'A Kensington Vespers'
Chesterton: G.K. Chesterton (1874–1936), author of *The Man Who Was Thursday* (novel) and *Lepanto* (poem), as well as the recently televised *Father Brown* stories. Frankie Howerd (1917–92), actor and comedian; *Up Pompeii* (1971) his funniest series.

'Of Paradise'
The Smith of Smiths: the Rev. Sidney Smith (1771–1845), Whig clergyman, moral philosopher and wit, who told a modest female Yorkshire parishioner that heaven was like eating pâté de foie gras to the sound of trumpets.

'Primavera for Pembroke Gardens'
St Mary Abbot's: high-spired Victorian parish church at the top of Kensington High Street.

'Winter Song'
The quotation in stanza seven is from Chapter One of *The Wind in the Willows*.

Title poem written in 2009; most of the others before 2000. The last poem in this section, 'Angela's Dream', is reprinted from my *Third Day: New and Selected Poems* (2008) as it reads best with other occasional verses. Prof. Dr Karl-Heinz Boher, author and critic, former editor of the German intellectual magazine *Merkur*, is married to my sister-in-law, Angela Bielenberg.

'Ballade Tragique'
In the 1990s I was a quangocrat. 'Quango' stands for Quasi Autonomous Non Governmental Organisation. Mine was the Arts Council of England. The ACE had just been made a beneficiary of untold National Lottery millions. Unfortunately, the rules governing their distribution had been drawn up by HM Treasury, not the Department of National Heritage (now the Department of Culture, Media and Sport), which was the government ministry sponsoring the Arts Council. So the Arts Council and its sponsors were locked in frequent and frustrating disagreements as to which arts organisations could receive money and for what purposes. In 1996, worn out by some of these tensions, I escaped for a long weekend to Ireland and vented my fury in the tragic ballad. I have cleaned it up a lot but it still rather slanders two revered individuals, the then Cultural Secretary and her Permanent Secretary. My apologies, for they were no doubt having an equally hard time themselves. Early this century, the succeeding administration sorted out the mess, which required primary legislative change. It did so at the cost of pinching some of the arts' money. Heigh ho. Throughout my public life, *Private Eye* occasionally depicted me as a golliwog, as I had dark frizzy hair and wore a bow tie. This designation is now considered politically incorrect.

'The Bidden Guest' (1986)
Vivien: Dame Vivien Duffield (1946–), philanthropist.
Metcalfe: David Metcalfe (1927–2012), insurance broker and investment banker.
Mavroleon: Bluey Mavroleon (1927–2009), Anglo-Greek shipowner.
Judy Taubman (1943–): wife of A. Alfred Taubman, in 1986 the proprietor of Sotheby's.
Lord Sieff: Marcus Sieff (1913–2001), a pillar of Marks & Spencer.
Kathy Ford (1949–): in 1986, wife of Henry Ford II.
Lord Lichfield (1939–2005): photographer.
Hedgecoe: John Hedgecoe (1932–2010), photographer and Professor of Photography at the Royal College of Art.
Fiona Allsopp (1947–): wife of Charles Allsopp, now Lord Hindlip (1940–), in 1986 London Chairman of Christie's; decorator; mother

of TV's Kirstie Allsopp.

Henries. On the cruise was Henry Ford II (1917–87), automobile manufacturer.

Philip Harari (1935–): art dealer.

Aliai Forte (1966–): wife of Sir Rocco Forte (*q.v.*, 1945–) hotelier; philanthropist.

Theresa Sackler: Dame Theresa Sackler, wife at the time of the cruise, now widow, of philanthropist Mortimer Sackler (1916–2010), philanthropist.

Jackie Stewart: Sir Jackie Stewart (1939–), motor racing champion.

Jocelyn: Sir Jocelyn Stevens (1932–), publisher and former Rector of the Royal College of Art. At the time of the cruise, partner of Vivien Duffield.

Roger Moore: Sir Roger Moore (1927–), actor and former James Bond.

Harry Fitzgibbons (1941–): entrepreneur.

Johnny Menzies: John Menzies (1926–2007), pronounced 'Ming-ies', pillar of John Menzies, newsagents.

Eck McEwen: Alexander McEwen (1935–2009), singer and stationer.

Sherwood: James Sherwood (1933–), pillar of Sea Containers and the Orient Express.

George Weidenfeld: Lord Weidenfeld (1919–), publisher.

Gordon Getty (1934–): composer, former oil magnate.

Olga Polizzi (1949–): hotelier, sister of Rocco Forte, now married to William Shawcross.

Maureen: Maureen Swanson (1932–2011), actress and film star married to Billy (*q.v.*).

Billy: The Earl of Dudley (1920–), gifted writer of occasional verse.

Sarah Hogg (1946–): following the cruise she became head of Prime Minister John Major's Policy Unit and later a corporation chairman. She sits in the House of Lords as Baroness Hogg and is also Viscountess Hailsham.

Sunny: The Duke of Marlborough (1926–), pillar of Blenheim; at the time of the cruise married to Rosita (*q.v.*).

Rosita: Rosita, Duchess of Marlborough (1943–), painter.

Rocco Forte: Sir Rocco Forte (1945–), hotelier.

Mr and Mrs Blond: Peter Blond (1932–), vintage car enthusiast and realtor, and his wife Virginia.

Charlie and Carol Price: at the time of the cruise, HE Charles Price (1931–2012) was US Ambassador to the Court of St James.

Gowrie and Allsopp: at the time of the cruise, the author (1939–) and Charles Allsopp (1940–), now Lord Hindlip, were the London chairmen of Sotheby's and Christie's respectively.

Tom Parr (1930–2011): interior designer.

Amabel: Lady Amabel Lindsay (living), interior designer.

Tessa: Tessa Kennedy (1938–), interior designer.

Lady Jane: Lady Jane Spencer-Churchill (1947–), interior designer.

Rhydian Morgan-Jones (1944–): racehorse breeder.

Edgar de P.: Edgar de Picciotto (living), Swiss banker.

Jacob R.: Lord Rothschild OM (1936–), financier and philanthropist.

Benson: Charles Benson (1935–2002), racing correspondent and gambler.

Ritblat: Sir John Ritblat (1935–), property developer and philanthropist.

Weinberg: Sir Mark Weinberg (1931–), financier and insurance magnate.

A small window on what used to be called café society, in the 1980s. So many gone into the world of light.

Acknowledgements

Thanks are due to the editors of *Agni*, *Agenda*, *The London Magazine*, *The New Statesman*, *PN Review*, *The Spectator*, *Standpoint* and *The Times Literary Supplement*, where some of the poems in this book first appeared.

The Andrians was published in a limited edition by Thomas Gibson Fine Art Limited and I am grateful to Thomas Gibson for its supervision. *Nursery Rhyme for Ninety* and *A Ballad of Bo-oz and Ruth* were published as pamphlets by The Greville Press and I would like to thank Anthony Astbury for his help and encouragement.

I am also indebted to the Calouste Gulbenkian Foundation; the Hawthornden Literary Institute; Wolfson College, Oxford; and the Legatum Institute for their support. I want to thank friends Lucy De Nardi, Rob Dick, Meinir Jones and Vishaile Patel for helping prepare *The Italian Visitor* and Helen Tookey of Carcanet for editing it.